How to Draw the Life and Times of
Richard M. Nixon

Lewis K. Parker

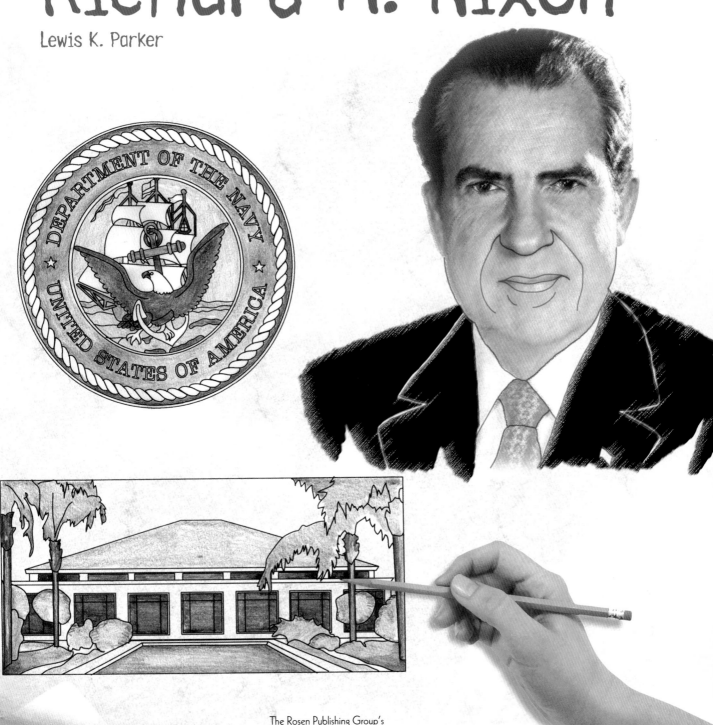

The Rosen Publishing Group's
PowerKids Press™
New York

This book is dedicated to my family, especially to Dakota, Tyrus, and Nicholas.

Published in 2006 by The Rosen Publishing Group, Inc.
29 East 21st Street, New York, NY 10010

First Edition

Editor: Melissa Acevedo
Layout Design: Julio A. Gil
Photo Researcher: Amy Feinberg

Illustrations: All illustrations by Albert B. Hanner.
Photo Credits: p. 4 © Topham/The Image Works; p. 7 © Wally McNamee/Corbis; pp. 8, 9, 26 Garren
Zuck/presidentialavenue.com; p. 10 (top) © Leng/Leng/Corbis; pp. 10 (bottom), 16, 20, 24 (bottom) ©
Bettmann/Corbis; p. 12 © Hulton Archive/Getty Images; p. 14 U.S. Navy; pp. 18, 24 (top) © AP/Wide World
Photos; p. 22 (top) Library of Congress Prints and Photographs Division, (bottom) © Royalty-Free/Corbis; p. 28 The
White House/Getty Images.

Library of Congress Cataloging-in-Publication Data

Parker, Lewis K.
How to draw the life and times of Richard M. Nixon / Lewis K. Parker.— 1st ed.
p. cm. — (A kid's guide to drawing the presidents of the United States of America) Includes index.
ISBN 1-4042-3013-0 (library binding)
1. Nixon, Richard M. (Richard Milhous), 1913– —Juvenile literature. 2. Presidents—United States—Biography—
Juvenile literature. 3. Drawing—Technique—Juvenile literature. I. Title. II. Series.
E856.P345 2006
973.924'092—dc22

2005017811

Printed in China

Contents

From Small-town Boy to President

Richard M. Nixon was the thirty-seventh president of the United States. Nixon was born on January 9, 1913, in a small town called Yorba Linda in southern California. He was the second of five sons. Nixon's father was a farmer, and his mother was a member of the  Quaker religion. This meant that Nixon was raised according to Quaker beliefs, which included settling arguments peacefully and avoiding dancing.

In 1922, when Nixon was nine, his family moved to Whittier, California, 15 miles (24 km) from Los Angeles. Nixon attended Whittier High School, where he did well academically, especially in history, his favorite subject. He also played violin and worked in his family's grocery store on the weekends. In 1930, Nixon entered Whittier College. He graduated in 1934, and studied law at Duke University Law School in Durham, North Carolina. In 1937, he returned to Whittier to practice law. In 1938, Nixon joined the Republican Party, which supported lower taxes.

In 1941, the United States entered World War II after Japan attacked the U.S. naval base at Pearl Harbor, Hawaii. As a Quaker Nixon was against war, but he joined the U.S. Navy in 1942 to help his country. When the war ended in 1945, Nixon began his political career. In 1946, he was elected to the U.S. House of Representatives. In 1950, Nixon was elected as a U.S. senator from California. He became vice president of the United States in 1953, and ran for president in 1960. He lost that election but was finally elected president in 1968.

You will need the following supplies to draw the life and times of Richard M. Nixon:

✓ A sketch pad   ✓ An eraser   ✓ A pencil   ✓ A ruler

These are some of the shapes and drawing terms you need to know:

Horizontal Line	——	Squiggly Line	∿
Oval	⬭	Trapezoid	▱
Rectangle	▭	Triangle	△
Shading		Vertical Line	|
Slanted Line	/	Wavy Line	∼

President Richard Nixon

   Richard Nixon's major goal as president was to end the Vietnam War. The war had started in the 1950s when Communist North Vietnam attacked South Vietnam. America had sent troops to aid South Vietnam in 1965. Many people were against this action. After the loss of many American soldiers, Nixon managed to bring the troops home. A treaty ended America's part in the war in January 1973.

   Nixon was reelected in 1972. Soon after, his troubles began. In 1973, his vice president resigned after being accused of dishonesty. In 1972, five men had broken into the Democratic headquarters at the Watergate Hotel in Washington, D.C. The men had been paid by a Nixon reelection committee to place hidden microphones inside the headquarters. Nixon said he knew nothing about the break-in, but the Senate discovered he was lying. On August 9, 1974, he resigned before he could be impeached. On April 22, 1994, Nixon died from a stroke in New York City.

One of Nixon's goals as president was to spread peace across the world. This picture of President Nixon was taken during his February 1972 trip to China. He met with Chinese premier Chou En-lai, seen here on the left, to talk about how China could trade peacefully with America.

Richard Nixon's California

California

Map of the United States of America

Richard Nixon was born in this house in Yorba Linda, California.

By the time Richard M. Nixon was born in southern California in 1913, the state's population had grown to 2.4 million people. Today California has the largest population in the United States with more than 35 million people living there.

The heavily populated state has found many ways to honor Nixon. The Richard Nixon Library and Birthplace is located in Yorba Linda, California, the small town where Nixon was born. The site, which is open to visitors, is maintained through the support of people and various companies. The 52,000-square-foot (4,831 sq m) museum holds many of the president's letters and speeches. It also has exhibits about the lives of Nixon and his wife, Pat.

Richard and Pat Nixon are buried in the Memorial Garden, outside the library. Just steps from the graves is the five-room house that Nixon's father built for his family in 1912. The house has been remodeled to look the way it did when Nixon lived there with his parents. Most of the furniture, such as the dining table and rocking chair, are the same ones the Nixon family used.

Nixon was buried in his hometown, Yorba Linda, California. His gravestone, shown above, is marked with the words, "The greatest honor history can bestow is the title of peacemaker." "Bestow" means "to give."

The Childhood of a President

Future president Richard M. Nixon was born on January 9, 1913, in Yorba Linda, California. In 1922, the family moved to Whittier, California, where Nixon's father opened a gas station and a grocery store. Nixon grew up as a member of the Quaker religion. He went to Quaker meetings four times on Sundays and again on Wednesday evenings. He also worked in his family's store before school and on weekends.

At Whittier High School, Nixon worked hard and earned outstanding grades. He also took part in school activities. He played sports, acted in various school plays, and was a member of the debate team. He also played the violin, like the one shown in the picture above, in his school's orchestra. When Nixon graduated from high school in 1930, he received awards that honored him as one of the best students in California.

1 Begin your drawing of the violin with a tall rectangle. Add a line in the left part of the box. Add two horizontal lines as shown. You should now have a box with four rectangles inside.

2 Add a long curved shape to the rectangle on the left for the bow. Note the part that sticks out at the top. Add two ovals to the middle rectangle on the right. The top oval is smaller than the bottom oval.

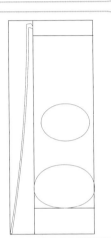

3 Draw two curved lines as shown to connect the ovals. Draw the shape at the bottom of the bow as shown. Add a long curved line from the top of the bow to the bottom for the bow's string.

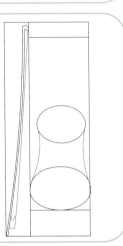

4 Draw two trapezoids as shown. The bottom one goes through the top oval. Use the oval guides to draw the shape of the violin. Add a V to the bottom oval. Add a curved line to the V.

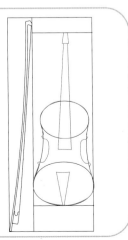

5 Erase all the extra lines from steps 1 through 4.

6 Draw two S shapes in the middle of the violin. Add a rectangle between them. Add the line below the left S. Add the two shapes to the violin's top. Below that add four pegs as shown.

7 Add the strings to the violin as shown. There are four strings.

8 Finish your drawing of the violin by shading it. Great work!

Meet Pat Nixon

In 1930, Richard M. Nixon entered Whittier College. When he graduated in 1934, he attended Duke University School of Law in Durham, North Carolina. After graduating from Duke in 1937, he returned to Whittier to work as a lawyer. In his spare time, Nixon acted in community plays. That was how he met his future wife, Thelma Catherine Ryan, who was nicknamed Pat.

In 1912, Pat was born in Ely, Nevada, where her father worked in a mine. When Pat was very young, her family moved to a farm near Los Angeles, California. In 1931, Pat moved to New York and worked as a secretary. She returned to California in 1934, and entered the University of Southern California, where she studied business and education.

Pat worked hard to pay for college. She graduated in 1937 and took a teaching job at Whittier High School in Whittier, California. Nixon and Pat fell in love, and they married on June 21, 1940.

1

Draw a large rectangle. It will be the guide for your drawing of Pat Nixon.

2

Draw an oval for her body. Add two circles for her shoulders. Draw an oval for her face. Then draw two circles for her eyes and one circle for her nose. Add a straight line for her mouth.

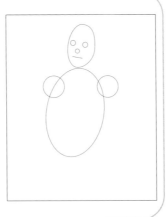

3

Draw the outline of Pat Nixon's hair. Then draw the outline of her body and her legs. Add three ovals for the arm in her lap. Draw two ovals and a circle for the arm resting on the chair.

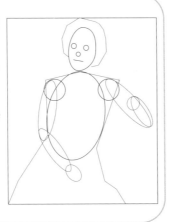

4

Draw the shape of her hair. Then draw the shapes of her face and her neck. Add the shapes of her nose, her two eyes, and her two lips. Add circles to each eye. Add lines to her face as shown.

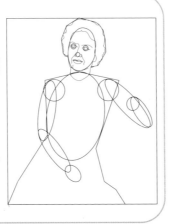

5

Use squiggly lines to draw her skirt and jacket. Make sure to draw her collar, her sleeves, and the line down the front of her jacket. Then add her hands as shown.

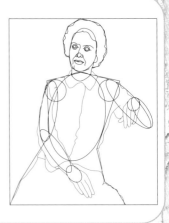

6

Draw circles and ovals for the buttons on her coat. Look closely at the picture and draw the back of the chair with wavy lines. Then add the sleeve of the arm resting on the chair.

7

Erase all the guides. Add small circles for Pat Nixon's earring, her necklace, and her ring. Use wavy lines to add details to the chair. Add more wavy lines for folds in her clothes.

8

Now you are ready to shade your drawing of Pat Nixon. The darkest parts are her eyes, her lips, her hair, and her skirt. Parts of the chair are also dark.

13

War and Politics

Richard M. Nixon's life changed soon after he married Pat. There had been a war going on in Europe since 1939. Germany had been attacking various countries and forming alliances with other countries, like Japan, to create an empire. America entered the war when Japan attacked a U.S. naval base at Pearl Harbor in Hawaii, on December 7, 1941. Nixon joined the U.S. Navy in August 1942. The Navy seal is shown above. For most of the war, he served in the Pacific.

After the war ended in 1945, Nixon continued to serve in the navy until 1946. Then the Republican Party chose him as their candidate for the U.S. House of Representatives. Nixon's campaign theme was that a vote for Nixon was a vote against Communism. At the time people feared that Communist governments would take over the world. Nixon used this fear in his bid for election by claiming that his opponent was swayed by Communism. On November 5, 1946, Nixon won, beginning his career in politics.

1

Draw a big circle. Add five smaller circles inside it as shown. The three circles on the outside are very close together. The two circles on the inside are also close together.

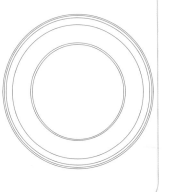

2

Add two more circles around the two smallest circles. Inside the smallest circle draw the outline of an eagle. Then use lines and a circle to draw an anchor as shown.

3

Draw shapes for rope between the two circles as shown. Finish drawing the anchor. Add details to the eagle's wings, neck, and tail with squiggly lines. Add the eagle's beak, eye, and claws.

4

Erase all extra lines. Draw water below the eagle with wavy lines. Add slanted lines and triangles to the left of the eagle as shown. Add five shapes to the anchor as shown. Add five sails as shown.

5

Draw the three shapes on top of the sails. Add the bottom sail behind the eagle. Add a line to the water.

6

Draw the three flags at the top of the ship. Make sure to add the details to the middle flag as shown. Draw waves in the water using wavy lines.

7

Write the words "DEPARTMENT OF THE NAVY" and "UNITED STATES OF AMERICA" as shown. Separate the words with stars.

8

You are now ready to shade your drawing. The sails are white, but the rest of the boat is dark. The eagle and the top of the anchor are also dark.

The Hiss Case

Nixon joined Congress's House Un-American Activities Committee. It questioned people believed to be Communists. The committee was afraid these people were spies who might give secrets about America to the Soviet Union, which included present-day Russia.

In August 1948, Nixon listened as Whittaker Chambers told the committee he was a Communist. He also said that Alger Hiss, a U.S. government officer, was a spy who told him American secrets. Nixon received permission from the committee to question Hiss. Chambers supported his claims by telling the committee where to find proof. This proof was microfilm of secret U.S. government documents. It had been hidden in a pumpkin on Chambers's farm in Maryland, as shown above. Because of Nixon's efforts, Hiss was sentenced to five years in prison on January 25, 1950. Soon Nixon became famous.

1

You will be drawing a pumpkin from Whittaker Chambers's farm. Begin your drawing of the pumpkin with a rectangle.

2

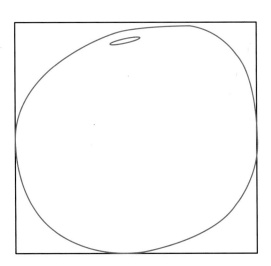

Draw the shape of the pumpkin inside the rectangle as shown. It looks a lot like a circle, but it is not perfectly round. Add a small oval at the top of the pumpkin.

3

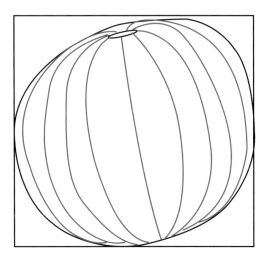

Draw nine curved lines from the top of the pumpkin to the bottom. Start in the middle and work your way to the sides. The closer to the middle the lines are, the less curved they are.

4

Erase the rectangular guide. You can now shade in your pumpkin. The sides are the darkest part.

From Senator to Vice President

In 1950, Richard M. Nixon was elected to the U.S. Senate. As a senator Nixon attacked the way President Truman had sent troops to fight against Communist North Korean forces in South Korea in 1948. Nixon wanted the troops to push into China and destroy the Communist government there.

In the 1952 presidential election, Nixon was chosen as Dwight Eisenhower's running mate. The picture above shows Nixon campaigning. However, after his candidacy was announced, a newspaper article claimed that Nixon had misused campaign money he received from businessmen. To clear his name of this and other charges, Nixon went on television. He said the money was used to pay for the campaign. Nixon and Eisenhower went on to win the election.

In 1960, after eight years of being vice president, Nixon ran for president but lost. When he lost the election for governor of California in 1962, Nixon announced that he was finished with politics.

1

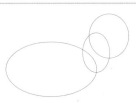

The picture on page 18 is of Nixon giving a speech in 1952. He is shown with two elephants because elephants stand for the Republican Party. Begin your elephant by drawing three ovals as shown.

2

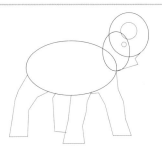

Draw the outlines of the elephant's four legs. Then draw the outline of the elephant's mouth. Add a small circle for the elephant's eye and a slightly larger circle for the inside of the elephant's trunk.

3

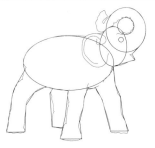

Use the guides to draw the elephant's trunk as shown. Add the elephant's ear with two curved lines. Then use the guides to draw the shape of the elephant's legs, its head, and its body.

4

Erase any extra lines. Use wavy lines to draw the elephant's tail and mouth as shown. Add wrinkles to the elephant's skin with more wavy lines.

5

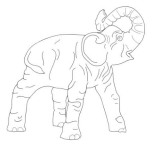

Use curved lines to add details to the elephant's feet and the end of its trunk. Add a small circle in the elephant's eye. Use curved lines to add wrinkles to the elephant's trunk and head as shown.

6

You have finished drawing the Republican elephant. You can now shade it. Outstanding work!

President Richard Nixon

In 1968, Richard M. Nixon returned to politics and decided to run for president with Spiro Agnew as his running mate. On November 5, 1968, Nixon  won the election. He immediately started working to improve life for Americans. He pushed three bills through Congress to help fight crime. In 1971, he supported the Twenty-sixth Amendment, which lowered the voting age to 18 for all elections.

At this time some school districts were segregated, even though laws forcing black and white students to go to different schools had been stopped in 1954. The U.S. Supreme Court ruled that communities could start busing students from one school to another to encourage integration. President Nixon did not think busing was a good idea, and he asked Congress to put a stop to it. Congress disagreed and the busing continued. Children from black neighborhoods, for example, were brought to schools in white neighborhoods on buses like the one shown above.

1

Begin your drawing of a school bus with a horizontal rectangle.

2

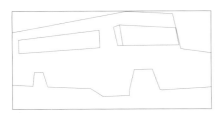

Look carefully at the drawing. Then use slanted lines to draw the outline of the bus. Draw three slanted shapes as shown for the windows.

3

Use the guides from step 2 to draw the shape of the bus. Use slanted lines to draw the door. Add lines to the right of the door. Draw two shapes on the door. Add shapes to the front and the back of the bus as shown.

4

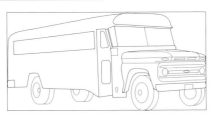

Erase all extra lines. Add ovals and curved lines for the bus's four wheels. Add curved and slanted lines to the front of the bus as shown. Draw shapes as shown to add more detail to the school bus.

5

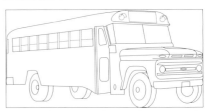

Draw a slanted rectangle and two circles on the front of the bus as shown. Add shapes to the circles as shown. Use slanted lines to add details to the windows and the door. Draw one more window at the back of the bus.

6

Add lines that curve around the holes for the wheels. Then draw nine slanted lines on the side of the school bus.

7

Erase the rectangular guide from step 1. Write the words "SCHOOL BUS" on the front of the bus as shown.

8

Your drawing of the school bus is done. Finish it with shading. The windows and some parts of the front of the bus do not need to be shaded. Great work!

The Vietnam War

In 1965, the U.S. government sent forces to help South Vietnam protect itself against the North. Many Americans were against this. The North Vietnamese flag is shown at right.

In June 1969, President Nixon announced that U.S. forces would start leaving South Vietnam. However, in April 1970, Nixon said troops had been sent into Cambodia, a nation bordering South Vietnam, to destroy North Vietnamese forces there. Many people were angry with Nixon. The political cartoon above depicts the president refusing to let go of Vietnam. On June 29, 1970, U.S. troops left Cambodia. By the end of 1972, there were fewer than 25,000 soldiers in South Vietnam. On January 27, 1973, an agreement to end the war was signed in Paris, France. In March 1973, Nixon welcomed home the last U.S. soldiers coming from Vietnam.

1

The picture on page 22 is a cartoon of Nixon holding a locked box of Vietnamese votes. Begin your drawing of the cartoon with a rectangle.

2

Draw a curved line across the rectangle as shown. Draw the guides for the feet as shown. Add the shape between the feet. It looks like a rectangle, but two of the sides are not straight.

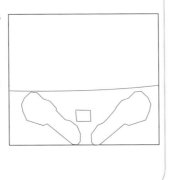

3

Use the guides to draw the feet as shown. Add an oval inside the shape between the feet. Add a small rectangle above the shape. Add slanted, horizontal, and curved lines as shown.

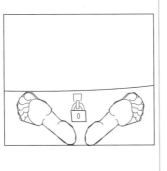

4

Erase the guides for the feet. Draw three slightly curved horizontal lines as shown. Draw eight slanted lines to make the top of the box. Add four slanted lines for the box's sides.

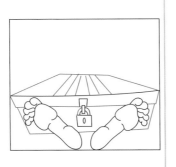

5

Draw the shape of Nixon's head. Start with the ears and work down on each side. Then draw the top of his head with squiggly lines. Add the shapes for his two eyes and his nose as shown.

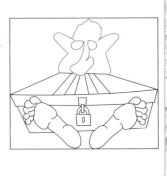

6

Draw Richard Nixon's hands. You can see four fingers on each hand. Add the curved lines for his ears as shown. Add details to his eyes and his nose as shown.

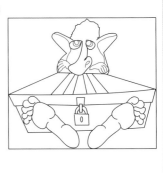

7

Erase the rectangular guide. Draw the shapes for Nixon's eyebrows. Add squiggly lines for his hair and the wrinkle in his forehead. Add the short line between his hand and his nose.

8

You can now shade in your drawing. The darkest parts are Nixon's hair, his arms, and the stripes on the box. Great job!

A Second Term and the Watergate Scandal

In 1972, Richard M. Nixon was elected for a second term. Soon after, Vice President Agnew was accused of not paying taxes. He resigned. Then Nixon faced the Watergate scandal.

In June 1972, five men paid by the Nixon reelection committee had broken into the Watergate Hotel. This was the location of the Democratic Party headquarters in Washington, D.C. The men had been caught planting secret microphones in the hotel. Nixon claimed that he did not know about the break-in. In July 1974, the Supreme Court ordered Nixon to turn over the White House conversations that were taped on the tape recorder above. The tapes showed Nixon knew about the break-in. The U.S. House of Representatives planned for Nixon's impeachment. On August 9, 1974, Nixon resigned and Vice President Gerald Ford became president. Ford pardoned his crimes within one month.

1

Nixon used the tape recorder on page 24 to record the talks he had with people while he was in the White House. Begin your drawing of the tape recorder with a rectangle.

2

Use slanted lines to draw the shape as shown. The line on the right is a little longer than the line on the left. This will be the lid of the tape recorder.

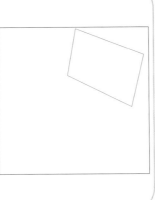

3

Draw the shape in the bottom half of the guide rectangle as shown. The short right side is longer than the short left side. Add slanted lines as shown to finish the shape of the tape recorder.

4

Add slanted lines to the tape recorder's lid as shown. Draw the shape in the middle of the lid. Draw the tape recorder's handle. Make sure to draw the lines along the edge of the handle as shown.

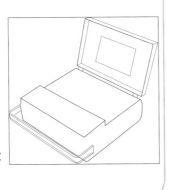

5

Erase the rectangular guide. Add five slanted rectangles as shown. Add 11 slanted lines as shown. Make sure that the top line on the side of the tape recorder curves at one end.

6

Draw 10 ovals as shown on the top, the front, and the side of the tape recorder. Add curved lines to the ovals on the top and the front of the tape recorder. Add slanted lines and shapes.

7

Add three ovals and six rectangles as shown. Add details to the big oval. Draw two lines from the big oval to the smaller oval next to it. Add the shape in the smaller oval.

8

Shade in your drawing of Nixon's tape recorder. Note that there are some parts that should be left white.

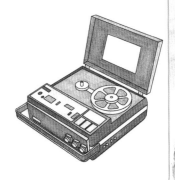

The Death of Richard Nixon

During the 20 years after the Watergate scandal, Richard M. Nixon tried to rebuild his standing in the  United States. He never again held a job in the U.S. government. However, he gave speeches and wrote books about his experiences in the government. He traveled to many countries and spoke to world leaders who respected him. He also advised later presidents about world events.

In 1990, the Richard Nixon Library, shown above, opened in Yorba Linda, California. Most of the living presidents of the United States attended the opening to show their respect for Nixon. He continued to travel the world, giving speeches to leaders and to college students who were interested in his presidency. On April 18, 1994, Richard Nixon suffered a stroke and died four days later in a hospital in New York City. He had just returned from a trip to the Soviet Union and had finished writing his eleventh book. He was 81 years old.

1

Start your drawing of the Richard Nixon Library with a long rectangular guide.

2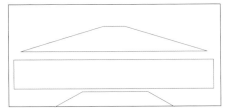

Draw a long rectangle in the bottom part of the rectangular guide. Add a horizontal line and two vertical lines under the rectangle. Draw a trapezoid above the rectangle as shown.

3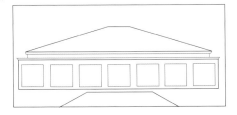

Draw seven squares in the rectangle. Draw a horizontal line just below the trapezoid and another one just above the rectangle. Add short slanted and vertical lines as shown.

4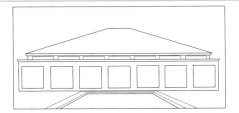

Add horizontal and vertical lines as shown between the horizontal lines from step 3. Add two horizontal lines and four slanted lines as shown. The horizontal lines are very close together.

5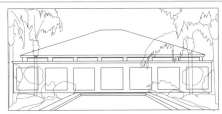

Use seven slightly slanted vertical lines to draw the trunks of the palm trees. Use squiggly lines to add the top parts of the trunks and the leaves. Then draw the grass and bushes as shown.

6

Erase all the lines of the building and the pool edge that are inside the plant shapes.

7

Add a square just inside each of the seven squares from step 3. These are the windows. Add one horizontal line and two vertical lines to each window. Do not draw the parts of the windows that are behind the bushes.

8

You are ready to shade in your picture of the library. The windows are the darkest part of the drawing.

Remembering Richard Nixon

By the time Richard M. Nixon died, many people had forgiven him for his crimes. President Bill Clinton ordered that all government offices close on the day of Nixon's funeral. Flags on government buildings were flown at half-mast. Nixon's coffin was taken from  New York City to California. The coffin was then placed in the Nixon Library in Yorba Linda, California. More than 40,000 people stood in line to view his body.

Richard Nixon had a long and important political career. He was elected twice as vice president and twice as president. He was the first U.S. president to visit China and start friendly relations with this Communist country. He ended U.S. involvement in the Vietnam War. He made a treaty with the Soviet Union to reduce the number of nuclear weapons. He will be remembered for his hard work in trying to bring peace to the entire world.

1

Begin your drawing of President Richard Nixon by drawing a rectangular guide.

2

Draw an oval as a guide for Nixon's head. Add two lines for his shoulders as shown.

3

Draw two lines below the oval as shown. Draw a curving line outside of the oval for his hair. Add a wavy line to show where his hair meets his face. Draw the shapes for his two ears.

4

Draw two circles as guides for his eyes. Add three more circles as guides for his nose. The middle circle should be a bit bigger than the other two circles. Add a wavy line for his mouth.

5

Use the eye guides to add his eyebrows and his eyes as shown. Use the nose guides to add his nose. Add wavy lines to his mouth. Add lines to his ears and his face. Draw the outline of his jaw.

6

Erase all extra lines. Draw lines to make the collar of Nixon's jacket. Add the shape for the pin as shown. Add wavy lines for his shirt collar and his tie.

7

Draw small circles in his eyes as shown. Add wavy lines for wrinkles to his neck, his forehead, his cheeks, and the area between his eyes.

8

Shade in your drawing of Richard Nixon. His tie and his eyebrows should be the darkest parts of the drawing.

Timeline

1913 Richard M. Nixon is born on January 9, in Yorba Linda, California.

1922 The Nixon family moves to Whittier, California.

1930 Nixon graduates from Whittier High School.

1934 Richard Nixon graduates from Whittier College.

1937 After graduating from Duke University Law School, Nixon becomes a lawyer in Whittier.

1940 Thelma Catherine Ryan, nicknamed Pat, and Nixon marry on June 21.

1942-1946 Nixon serves in the U.S. Navy.

1946 Richard Nixon is elected to the U.S. House of Representatives.

1948 Nixon is reelected to the U.S. House of Representatives.

1950 Richard Nixon is elected to the U.S. Senate.

1953-1961 Nixon serves as vice president to President Eisenhower.

1960 Richard M. Nixon runs for president of the United States. He loses to John F. Kennedy.

1962 Nixon loses the election for governor of California.

1968 Nixon is elected the thirty-seventh president of the United States.

1969 Nixon announces the beginning of the withdrawal of U.S. troops from South Vietnam.

1972 Nixon visits China, becoming the first U.S. president to do so.
Five men break into the Watergate Hotel on June 17.
Nixon is reelected president.

1973 Vice President Spiro Agnew resigns on October 10. Gerald Ford becomes the new vice president.

1974 White House tapes come out indicating Nixon as part of a cover-up of the Watergate scandal on August 5.
Nixon resigns and Ford becomes the thirty-eighth president on August 9.

1994 Richard M. Nixon dies in New York City on April 22.

Glossary

alliances (uh-LY-unts-ez) Groups of countries working together toward a common goal.

awards (uh-WORDZ) Things that are given after careful thought.

candidate (KAN-dih-dayt) A person who runs in an election.

coffin (KAH-fun) A box that holds a dead body.

committee (kuh-MIH-tee) A group of people directed to oversee or to consider a matter.

Communist (KOM-yuh-nist) Belonging to a system in which the government owns all property and goods, which are shared equally by everyone.

conversations (kon-ver-SAY-shunz) Talking.

debate (dih-BAYT) Having to do with a meeting at which people or groups argue different points of view.

Democratic (deh-muh-KRA-tik) Having to do with one of the two major political parties in the United States.

future (FYOO-chur) Having to do with the time that is coming.

impeached (im-PEECHD) Removed from office because of misconduct.

integration (in-tuh-GRAY-shun) The act of bringing together different races or social classes.

involvement (in-VOLV-ment) Taking part.

lawyer (LOY-er) A person who gives advice about the law and who speaks for people in court.

microfilm (MY-kruh-film) Pictures of printed matter that can be viewed with a special machine.

microphones (MY-kruh-fohnz) Instruments used to record sounds or to make sounds louder.

nuclear weapons (NOO-klee-ur WEH-punz) Very strong weapons that are sometimes used in times of war.

orchestra (OR-kes-truh) A group of people who play music together.

pardoned (PAR-dund) Excused someone who did something wrong.

resigned (rih-ZYND) Stepped down from a position.

scandal (SKAN-dul) Conduct that people find shocking and bad.

segregated (SEH-gruh-gayt-ed) Separated by race.

site (SYT) The place where a certain event happens.

Soviet Union (SOH-vee-et YOON-yun) A former country that reached from eastern Europe across Asia to the Pacific Ocean.

Supreme Court (suh-PREEM KORT) The highest court in the United States.

Index

Web Sites

Due to the changing nature of Internet links, PowerKids Press has developed an online list of Web sites related to the subject of this book. This site is updated regularly. Please use this link to access the list:
www.powerkidslinks.com/kgdpusa/nixon/